Teaching
Children
Bible Basics

TEACHING

Children
Bible Basics

34 LESSONS
That Help Kids Learn to Use the Bible

Barbara Bruce

ABINGDON PRESS
Nashville

TEACHING CHILDREN BIBLE BASICS:
THIRTY-FOUR LESSONS THAT HELP KIDS LEARN TO USE THE BIBLE

Copyright © 1999 by Abingdon Press

All rights reserved.

This book is printed on recycled, acid-free paper.

Library of Congress Cataloging-in-Publication Data

Bruce, Barbara.
    Teaching children Bible basics : 34 lessons that help children learn to use the Bible / Barbara Bruce.
       p. cm.
    Includes index.
    ISBN 0-687-02465-X (alk. paper)
    1. Bible—Children's use.   2. Bible—Study and teaching (Elementary)—Activity programs.   3. Christian education of children.   I. Title.
    BS618.B78   1999
    268'.432—dc21   99-39689
                                                                    CIP

Scripture quotations, unless otherwise indicated, are from the New Revised Standard Version Bible, copyright © 1989, by the Division of Christian Education of the National Council of the Churches of Christ in the United States of America.

Permission to reproduce pages 21, 27, 28, 33, 36, 41, 45, 48, 51, 54-58, 65, 70, 77, 80, 85-86, 91, 96, 99, 100, 109, 112, 115, 119, and 120-23 is granted to purchasers of this book.

99 00 01 02 03 04 05 06 07 08—10 9 8 7 6 5 4 3 2 1

MANUFACTURED IN THE UNITED STATES OF AMERICA

To Kathy
whose love, laughter, and support
made this book possible
and whose ministry
will touch many lives.

Contents

PART 3
The Christian/New Testament Teaches Us How to Live

Preface

Several years ago a newly appointed Christian educator and the pastor took their confirmation class to a service in a synagogue. After the service the rabbi held a special session for this class. She took down the Torah so the class could see it up close. She asked this class of seventh graders, "Who can tell me the books of the Torah?" The students carefully examined the floor, the ceiling, and their fingernails. The pastor and the Christian educator wanted to crawl under the nearest chair. It was an embarrassing moment for all. The Christian educator vowed that this would never happen again.

Unfortunately, this is not an unusual occurrence. Students who have regularly attended Sunday school sometimes do not know much about the Bible. In fact, many adults today do not know much about the Bible. *Teaching Children Bible Basics* is an attempt to turn the trend around. This book is a resource that can be used in an after-school program, as a special curriculum for the third (or fourth) grade, a special time apart after the Children's Time, or in a variety of ways determined by your time, needs, and creative imagination. Learn with and from the children. Their insights and questions will spark a new appreciation and understanding of the Bible. Enjoy!

Barbara Bruce

Introduction

Most churches present Bibles to children when they are in the third or fourth grade. We record the children's names, the date, and the name of the church. We gift-wrap the Bibles, have a special presentation, and tell the children to read them and bring them to their church school class. Period!

Teaching Children Bible Basics is an adventure, an exploration, a discovery, and a journey that will help children to become acquainted with this precious gift.

Teaching Children Bible Basics is fun, and it helps children to make the Bible their book. It is a how-to-use-the-Bible book—it is informational. It is also a book that will help children to experience major biblical stories in ways that relate to their lives today—it is formational.

I encourage you to read through the lessons and adapt them to your class members' needs by adding or subtracting ideas and activities where you see fit. Read at least one week ahead since you may need to gather special supplies, set up your room, or ask students to bring an item with them.

Teaching Children Bible Basics is designed for elementary aged children. At this stage of their faith development, children can be informed that:

- the Bible is divided into two parts
  —the Hebrew Bible/Old Testament, which contains

stories of God's creation and mighty acts and of early believers who knew God;

—the Christian Scriptures/New Testament, which contains stories of Jesus' life and teachings and of those who followed him;

- the Bible teaches us how to live with one another;
- the Bible is an account of the relationship between God and us;
- the Bible is our book for our present lives.

Teaching Children Bible Basics is based on the educational principles that children learn:

- through all of seven intelligences (i.e., verbal/linguistic, logical/mathematical, visual/spatial, body/kinesthetic, musical/rhythmic, interpersonal, intrapersonal);
- interactively;
- experientially;
- in an environment that is safe and comfortable;
- when they must search for an answer;
- in order to translate their learning to their lives and language;
- when their leader understands and cares about them;
- at different rates and ability levels.

Included in each lesson is a "Parents' Question." This is an effort to have parents become more involved in their child's learning. It becomes a family learning project. Inviting parents to sign a paper that says the question has been discussed and returning it to you helps to ensure participation.

We use *The New Adventure Bible.* Please select a Bible translation that is appropriate for the age level of your class. One that includes illustrations, maps, questions, and other information is essential to develop a child's understanding.

PART 1
The Bible

LESSON 1

In the beginning

Focus: In the beginning

Scripture: John 1:1

Connections: Students will experience counting the books of the Bible, discovering that the Bible is divided into two parts, and how the Bible came to be.

Materials Needed: 66 books (large/small/thick/thin/hymnal, etc.) arranged on a table that is easy for students to access, each student's Bible, newsprint/marker or chalkboard/chalk, parent signature slips.

Activities:

1. **Opening:** Share names, grades, schools attended, and favorite subject. Invite students to get to know each other's names and other helpful information. **Say: What is the Bible?** Invite discussion and record answers.

2. Invite students to count together the books that are arranged on the table. One child can point while the others count. Then ask them to open their Bibles to the table of contents and count the number of books listed. Share with students the fact that each of the books tells a special story of God's people. Some of the books are poetry,

songs (psalms), or laws, and some are letters; but all of the books give us information that helps us to know God.

3. Refer again to the table of contents. Ask students to discover the two main parts of the Bible. Look for the word *testament*—ask if anyone knows the meaning of "testament." Explain that "testament" means a covenant or promise between God and humans. The Old Testament tells us about how God created the world and the early stories of God and God's people. We will be learning about some important people who played a great part in who we are as God's children. Also, the New Testament is about Jesus' life and his teachings. Ask if any of them have friends who are Jewish. Explain that Jewish people refer to the first part of the Bible as the Hebrew Bible, rather than the Old Testament, and the second part of the Bible as the Christian Testament, rather than the New Testament. Ask the students why they think this is so. Invite discussion.

4. Ask students how they think the Bible came to be. Invite discussion. Explain that the Bible began by people's telling stories about God's part in their lives. They told these stories around campfires as a way of teaching their children about God. Play the game "telephone"—each person will pass on what he or she hears by whispering it once to the child next to them. Be sure to tell everyone that they can say the phrase only one time. Whisper into the first child's ear, "In the beginning was the Word and the Word was with God and the Word was God." When every child has received the message, ask the last child to repeat what he or she heard. Compare the ending message with the beginning message. Ask students what they think this activity has to do with the Bible. Tell them that

16

some of the stories may have gotten repeated differently, but the main story was pretty much the same. Some of the details may be exaggerated, but the story of the Bible is about God and how God acted in people's lives then and now.

5. *Closing:* Close with a prayer, thanking God for the gift of the Bible and for helping us learn how to use it and learn how God wants us to live.

Parents' Question: How many books are in the Bible? Give each student a slip for parents to sign.

LESSON 2

How do I use my Bible?

Focus: How do I use my Bible?

Scripture: John 8:12

Materials Needed: Bibles, a copy of the Bible Bookmark for each student (page 21), crayons or markers, newsprint/markers or chalkboard/chalk, parent signature slips.

Connections: Students will hear the scripture verse read aloud and discuss why Jesus is the light of the world and how the Bible helps us to "see" by this light. Students will discover a means of remembering the names of the first five books of the Bible, how to locate several books in the Bible, how to find specific chapters and verses, and they will create a personal Bible bookmark.

Activities:

1. *Opening:* Review Lesson 1 by asking how many books are contained in the Bible. Ask students how many of their parents knew there were 66 books in the Bible and how the Bible came to be. Collect parent signature slips.

2. Turn to the table of contents of the Bible. Ask students to name the first five books of the Bible as listed. Help them with pronunciation, if necessary. Tell them that Jewish

people refer to these books as the *Torah.* Explain that Torah means "teaching" and that the Torah is a record of God's covenant with human beings. Tell the students that covenant means "promise." **Say: We will learn about many covenants, or promises, between God and humans. We will keep a list of all the covenants we discover in the Bible.** Show students a scroll to illustrate that the Torah is a scroll that was written by hand on sheepskin or parchment paper and is very special. It is so special that it is kept in a sacred place in a Jewish temple or synagogue. Because the paper is so fragile, it is not touched by human hands; instead a special pointer is used to help read the verses. Invite students to create a song or rap to help them remember the books of the Torah. Ask them to practice their song or rap several times until they have it memorized.

3. Invite students to open their Bibles and look through them and make discoveries. **Say: Are there pictures or maps? What discoveries can you make?** Now ask them to find the first book of the Bible. Ask what the name of the first book is. Help them find Genesis 1:1. Point out the large number and tell them this is the chapter— Genesis 1—and that it is the first chapter in the book of Genesis. Next have them find the small number. Explain that this number is the first verse in the first chapter of Genesis. Ask them to keep these two numbers in mind and discover how many verses (small numbers) there are in Genesis, chapter 1. Help any students who appear lost, or if there are students who catch on quickly, ask them to help a friend. When all the students have discovered how many verses there are in Genesis 1, ask them how many chapters (big numbers) are in Genesis. Help them to make this discovery. Next, ask them to find the number of vers-

es (small number) in the book of Exodus, chapter 6. Turn to Leviticus and ask them the number of chapters (big number) in the book of Leviticus. Then ask how many verses (small number) there are in Numbers 14. Move to Deuteronomy and name the number of chapters (big number) that are included. If time permits, allow the students to suggest other chapters and verses from the Torah to locate.

4. Invite students to create a personal Bible bookmark. Have them print their names on the bookmark and draw a picture or symbol of what the Bible means to them.

5. *Closing:* Lead the students in a prayer, asking God to help them use the Bible to teach them how to know God.

Parents' Question: Do you know what the Torah is? What are the names of the first five books of the Bible? Give each student a slip for parents to sign.

BIBLE'S

BIBLE'S

BIBLE'S

BIBLE'S

PART 2

The Hebrew Bible/ Old Testament Teaches Us Today

LESSON 3

The story of creation

Focus: The story of creation

Scripture: Genesis 1:1–2:3

Connections: Students will read and retell the creation story day by day and discover ways they can protect and preserve God's creation.

Materials Needed: Bibles, copy of "God's Creation" (page 27), newsprint/markers or chalkboard/chalk, modeling clay, pencils, and "My Promise to Protect God's Earth" (page 28), parent signature slips.

Activities:

1. *Opening:* Say: **If you were creating the world, what would you make sure was included? What would you leave out?** Encourage discussion of things the students love best and those they consider "yucky," like snakes, mosquitoes, etc. Collect parent signature slips.

2. Invite students to find Genesis 1:1 in their Bibles. Ask for volunteers to read the creation story one day at a time. After each day, discuss briefly what was created. Distribute copies of "God's Creation." Encourage the students to draw a picture of what was created on each day.

25

3. Invite each student (or pairs of students, depending on the size of your group and your students' abilities) to select one day of creation and make an object from clay that will show what was created that day.

4. As students are creating their objects ask them to describe ways they can preserve and protect what God has created. Make a list of the various ways students can be caretakers of this world that God has given us. Then ask them to make a covenant by filling in and signing the "My Promise to Protect God's Earth" form, on which each student agrees to do something to protect God's earth.

5. *Closing:* Pray together, using Psalm 8:1, and thank God for creating all things, even us.

Parents' Question: What did God create on each day? Give each student a slip for parents to sign.

God's Creation

Day 1. God created day and night.

Day 2. God created the sky.

Day 3. God created land and seas and all the plants that grow on the land.

Day 4. God created the sun for day and the moon for night.

Day 5. God created all the living things in the sea and all the birds of the air.

Day 6. God created all the living things on the earth, including man and woman in God's image.

Day 7. God rested and called the day holy.

MY PROMISE TO PROTECT GOD'S EARTH

I promise to take care of God's creation by _____

_____

_____

Name _____

MY PROMISE TO PROTECT GOD'S EARTH

I promise to take care of God's creation by _____

_____

_____

Name _____

MY PROMISE TO PROTECT GOD'S EARTH

I promise to take care of God's creation by _____

_____

_____

Name _____

MY PROMISE TO PROTECT GOD'S EARTH

I promise to take care of God's creation by _____

_____

_____

Name _____

LESSON 4

Adam and Eve
and choices

Focus: Adam and Eve and choices

Scripture: Genesis 2:4–3:13

Connections: Students will hear the second creation story and discuss making choices.

Materials Needed: Bibles, newsprint/markers or chalkboard/chalk, paper, markers, pencils, a picture (from a Bible or picture file) of Adam and Eve in the Garden of Eden, parent signature slips.

Activities:

1. *Opening:* Ask students to tell about a time when they did something they wished they had not done. **Say: What happened because of what you did?** Create a chart of what students did and what happened because of their action. When all students who wish to tell their story have spoken, tell them they are going to hear a story about the first man and woman that God created, a very bad choice they made, and what happened because of it. Collect parent signature slips.

2. Engage the students as you tell the second story of creation—Genesis 2:4–3:13—in your own words, being sure

29

to use words and concepts that children will understand. As you tell the story, display the picture of Adam and Eve. Add suspense and animation as you tell the story. Ask frequently, "What do you think happened next?"

3. Add to your chart the actions Eve and Adam took and what happened because they disobeyed God. Invite answers from the students and record their words on the chart.

4. Ask students what they think the world would be like if Eve and Adam had never eaten the fruit. Talk with students about some of the things that would not be present in the world if everyone from Eve and Adam on down to us had obeyed God. Share the "peaceable kingdom" (Isaiah 11:6-9). Provide students with blank paper, markers, and pencils. Invite students to write about or draw what they think the world would look like if we all obeyed God always.

5. *Closing:* Help children to locate Isaiah 11:6 and read the "peaceable kingdom" in unison. Ask God for help in obeying God's rules.

Parents' Question: What did Eve and Adam do to disobey God? What happened because they disobeyed? Give each student a slip for parents to sign.

LESSON 5

God destroys the world—almost

Focus: God destroys the world—almost

Scripture: Genesis 6–9

Connections: Students will encounter the story of Noah and the great flood through a song and discover another covenant, parent signature slips.

Materials Needed: Newsprint/markers or chalk and chalkboard, copies of page 33 of this book for each student, markers or crayons.

Activities:

1. *Opening:* Ask students to think about what they would do if a tornado (or some other type of major storm) was coming in 30 minutes. Tell them they must prepare to leave and take all of their family members and pets with them. Stress that they will be leaving quickly and will have little time to pack. Ask what would they take with them. Allow time for discussion. Ask why they made the decisions they did. Ask if they know a story in the Bible that tells about God saving one family. Collect signature slips.

2. Ask students to tell you everything they know about Noah. Record their answers without comment on news-

print or chalkboard. Tell the story of Noah and the great flood in your own words or have someone come in costume and tell the story in first person. Ask the students to listen carefully for the covenant. As the story is told have a student place a checkmark next to each item on the list of things the class knew about Noah. Afterward check the list against the story. Ask them what the covenant was that God made with Noah.

3. Learn "The Noah Song." Teach the chorus and the tune. Invite the students to sing the song with you. Sing the chorus after every verse.

4. Once you have sung the song through once, sing it again and invite students to draw a quick picture on the newsprint or chalkboard to go along with each verse. Sing the song a third time using pictures to help remember the words.

5. On the back of the copy of "The Noah Song," suggest that students draw a rainbow and ask them to think of the closing verse about the promise that God made—God would never again destroy the world with a flood.

6. *Closing:* Finish with a prayer about God's making and keeping promises or covenants.

Parents' Question: What do you know about the story of Noah and the great flood? Give each student a slip for parents to sign.

The Noah Song

(Tune: Jesus Loves Me)

Noah built an ark we know
for the Bible tells us so.
God said, "It is gonna pour,
get those animals off the shore."

Chorus:
God had Noah save them.
God had Noah save them.
God had Noah save them.
The Bible tells us so.

Got those animals in his boat
Just as it began to float.
Forty days it floated 'round
Since there was no solid ground.

Then the sun began to shine.
Dried the land up mighty fine.
Sent a dove out, took a chance
She brought back an olive branch.

When Noah stepped on solid ground
Trees and bushes all around.
And a rainbow shone above.
God's promise shows his love.

LESSON 6
Abraham and Sarah and laughter

Focus: Abraham and Sarah and laughter

Scripture: Genesis 17:1-8, 15-17; 18:1-15; 21:1-7

Connections: Students will discover the importance of names in the Hebrew Bible, that God keeps the covenant, and that anything is possible with God.

Materials Needed: A book of names, a person to tell the story in first person or a tape of someone telling the story in first person, one copy of the "Father Abraham" song (page 36) for each child, parent signature slip. *Optional:* If you have someone in your congregation who is ninety or close to it, invite that person to come in and talk about how God has kept promises to him or her.

Activities:

1. *Opening:* **Say: What's in a name?** Ask students if they know how their names were chosen. Look up each student's name in the name book. Tell them what their names mean. Tell them that they are going to learn about another covenant that God made and about a child named "Laughter." Collect parent signature slips.

2. Ask students if they know someone who is ninety years

34

old. Talk about great-grandparents or someone in your congregation who may be that old. Ask them to think about this person having a baby. Tell them that in the book of Genesis God makes a promise to a man and his wife, but it takes many years to keep the promise. Have the guest tell (or play the tape of) the story of Abraham and Sarah in first person from Sarah's perspective. Ask the students to listen to the story, and then tell it in their own words. Invite one student to begin the story and tell a sentence or two. Then ask another student to tell the next part of the story. Continue the story until it is complete.

3. Ask students why they think Abraham and Sarah named their only son "Laughter." Ask what they think they would have done if God had made a promise to them and then took over sixty years to keep it. Would they give up hope? Would they no longer believe that God keeps God's word? Invite discussion.

4. Ask them if God has made a promise to us today. What is that promise? How do we know if God is keeping the promise?

5. Learn the song "Father Abraham." Go through the tune and words with the children. Then lead them in singing "Father Abraham," adding in the accompanying actions. If the tune is unfamiliar, create your own rhythm for the song and movements and sing it as a rap.

6. *Closing:* Offer a prayer about believing in God's promises.

Parents' Question: What was special about the baby named Isaac that was born to Abraham and Sarah? What does "Isaac" mean? Give each student a slip for parents to sign.

Father Abraham

Father Abraham had many sons
Many sons had Father Abraham
You are one of them and so am I
So let's all praise the Lord right hand
  (wave right hand)

sing the verse again with this ending
So let's all praise the Lord left hand
(wave left hand)

sing the verse again with this ending
So let's all praise the Lord right foot
(shake right foot)

sing the verse again with this ending
So let's all praise the Lord left foot
(shake left foot)

sing the verse again with this ending
So let's all praise the Lord nod you head
(nod your head)

sing the verse again with this ending
So let's all praise the Lord AMEN
(shout Amen)

LESSON 7

God has a plan for Joseph

Focus: God has a plan for Joseph

Scripture: Genesis 37:1-36

Connections: Students will review Joseph's dreams and his brothers' antagonism.

Materials Needed: Bibles, paper, pencils, newsprint/markers or chalkboard/chalk, parent signature slips.

Activities:

1. *Opening:* **Say: Have you ever felt that your parents played favorites with you and your brothers and sisters?** Encourage discussion and ask for outcomes. Tell students that in this lesson we are going to learn about a favorite son and how being the favorite got him into big trouble. Collect parent signature slips.

2. Invite students to locate Genesis 37. Ask them to read to themselves from 37:1-11 and then tell about the dreams that Joseph had. Allow discussion about how they believe Joseph's older brothers must have felt when he told them about his dreams.

3. Invite students to read the story of Joseph and his broth-

ers from Genesis 37:12-36. Ask them to write a letter to a friend as if they were Joseph telling about his experience. Allow enough time for reading and writing. Invite everyone to share letters with the class. (If your students have difficulty reading this much printed material, tell them the story or read it with expression.)

4. Give students the opportunity to play a *Pictionary*-type game in two teams. Ask them to add up their shoe sizes. The team with the largest shoe size goes first. Team 1 gets to choose a scene from the story of Joseph and draw it. Team 2 will have 2 minutes to guess what the scene is. If they guess correctly, they get to draw the next picture. If they do not guess correctly, Team 1 gets to draw another scene from the story. Play until both teams have had an opportunity to draw at least once or until you run out of time.

5. *Closing:* Invite the students to join in a prayer asking God to help you get along with brothers and/or sisters.

Parents' Question: Do you know the special gift that Joseph's father gave him? Give each student a slip for parents to sign.

LESSON 8
Ten Commandments

Focus: Ten Commandments

Scripture: Exodus 20:1-17

Connections: Students will read the Ten Commandments and create commandments (rules) for themselves.

Materials Needed: Bibles, newsprint/markers or chalkboard/chalk, one copy of the Ten Commandments (page 41) for each student, pencils, parent signature slips.

Activities:
1. *Opening:* Ask students to tell about one rule they have in their family. Record the rules on newsprint. Ask why each rule was made. Do the rules seem fair? Why do we need rules? Explain that we are going to learn some rules that God gave to the Israelites. Collect parent signature slips.

2. **Say: Many years after Joseph died, the Israelites who were living in Egypt became slaves. God was unhappy about the Israelites being slaves. God chose Moses to go and convince Pharaoh (another word for ruler or king) to let the people go. It took a long time and many years of sadness and disappointment, but finally Pharaoh agreed to let the Israelites leave Egypt.**

Moses led the Israelites across the Red Sea, and they wandered in the desert for forty years. The people became upset and angry with Moses. God gave Moses laws or rules for the way God wanted people to behave. The Ten Commandments are the rules God gave to Moses.

3. Invite students to find Exodus 20:1-17. Ask for volunteers to read the commandments. Explain each one after it is read. Ask if students think it is still a good rule for today.

4. Give each child a copy of the Ten Commandments. Have them turn the paper over and write the commandments they believe are most important for them.

5. **Closing:** Lead a prayer, asking God to help us obey God's rules.

Parents' Question: Can you name the Ten Commandments? Give each student a slip for parents to sign.

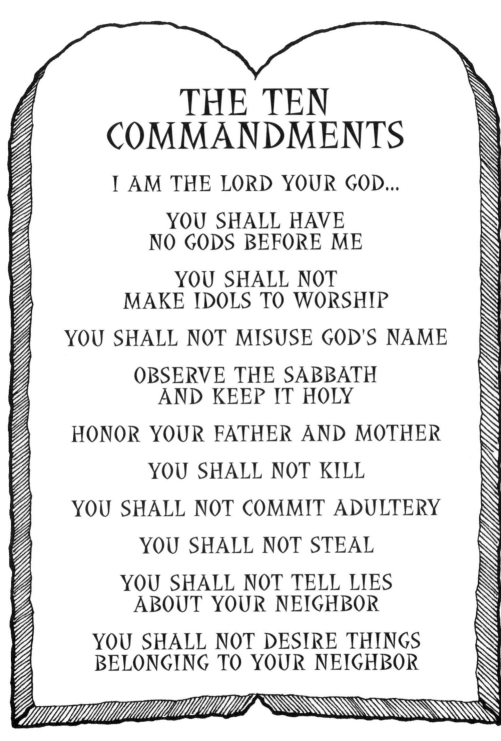

THE TEN COMMANDMENTS

I AM THE LORD YOUR GOD...

YOU SHALL HAVE
NO GODS BEFORE ME

YOU SHALL NOT
MAKE IDOLS TO WORSHIP

YOU SHALL NOT MISUSE GOD'S NAME

OBSERVE THE SABBATH
AND KEEP IT HOLY

HONOR YOUR FATHER AND MOTHER

YOU SHALL NOT KILL

YOU SHALL NOT COMMIT ADULTERY

YOU SHALL NOT STEAL

YOU SHALL NOT TELL LIES
ABOUT YOUR NEIGHBOR

YOU SHALL NOT DESIRE THINGS
BELONGING TO YOUR NEIGHBOR

LESSON 9

Children can do amazing things with God's help

Focus: Children can do amazing things with God's help

Scripture: 1 Samuel 17:4-9, 32-50

Connections: Students will read the story of David and Goliath and discover that God works through children like them.

Materials Needed: Bibles, shepherd's sling,* Ping-Pong balls, copies of "The Shepherd and the Sling" (page 45), markers, parent signature slips.

Activities:

1. *Opening:* **Say: Do you know a bully? Is there someone who is big, looks tough, frightens smaller kids, and tries to always get his or her own way?** Invite discussion. Ask students what they think is the best way to deal with a bully. Tell them that today we are moving

---

*If you cannot locate a shepherd's sling, you can create one by cutting a two-yard piece of twine in half (two equal pieces, one yard each). Obtain a piece of heavy fabric about three inches long and two inches wide. Gather one end of the fabric, accordian style, and tie it together with one of the pieces of twine. Do the same with the other end of fabric to create a pouch or pocket. Place a Ping-Pong ball in the pouch, hold the two ends of the sling, and begin spinning the sling rapidly. When you have gathered enough speed in spinning, raise the sling above your head and aim it toward one side of the room and use a throwing motion to release the Ping-Pong ball (stone). This will take lots of practice. If there is enough space in the room, allow students to practice. Be careful to provide close adult supervision.

many years ahead in the Bible history to meet a young shepherd boy who, with God's help, fought off a giant bully. Collect parent signature slips.

2. Show the students your sling. Demonstrate how to twirl it over your head.

3. Give a copy of the picture of "The Shepherd and the Sling" (page 45) to each student. Allow time for them to study the picture and ask questions. Then invite students to color the picture as you tell them this story: A young boy, maybe a little bit older than they are, is out on a rocky hillside watching over the sheep. See the sun shining down on him as he sits on a hillside. The sheep are all fine, and he picks up his sling—it is a long strand of cord with a small pouch in the middle. The boy selects a stone from a pile on the ground. He places the stone in the pouch of the sling and begins to twirl it over his head. Faster and faster the sling goes when he flings it out straight ahead. With amazing speed the stone leaves the sling and hits a tree about thirty feet away. Watch as the shepherd boy practices again and again with his sling. Finally he sits down to have his lunch, when he hears a huge roar. He quickly grabs his sling and a stone. He twirls the sling around his head and lets the stone fly straight at the lion that is coming toward one of his sheep. The stone hits the lion in the head and kills it. The boy and all of his sheep are safe. Invite students to tell you what their thoughts and feelings were as you had them listen and see this picture in their minds.

4. Explain who the Philistines were (enemies of Saul and the Israelites) and that Goliath was the bully who was part of the Philistine army who had the Israelite army fright-

ened. The Bible says that Goliath was six cubits (a "cubit" was a unit of measure from the elbow to the tip of the fingers—roughly eighteen inches) tall. Show them on the wall of the room or on the floor how tall that would be. Explain that David was a shepherd boy just like the picture they colored. He asked King Saul if he could go and fight the Philistine giant Goliath. Ask if they thought David was brave or dumb, then read from 1 Samuel 17:32-50, stopping to ask questions and receive feedback when appropriate.

5. *Closing:* Close with a prayer for believing that God is on our side when we are in trouble.

Parents' Questions: How big is a cubit? Do you think David was brave or dumb to fight Goliath? Give each student a slip for parents to sign.

The Shepherd and the Sling

LESSON 10
Songs to God

Focus: Songs to God

Scripture: Psalm 23

Connections: Students will learn what a psalm is and become familiar with a few of the Psalms.

Materials Needed: Bibles, copies of "The Psalms" (page 48), pencils, newsprint/markers or chalkboard/chalk, parent signature slips.

Activities:

1. *Opening:* Ask the students if they know a song that is sad. Ask if they know a song that is thankful. Ask if they know a praise song. Ask for their favorite praise song (if they do not know praise music, remind them of "Rise and Shine" from the Noah lesson). Sing a favorite praise song or "The Noah Song" (page 33). Collect parent signature slips.

2. Invite students to open their Bibles to the middle. Ask what book of the Bible they are in. (Individual psalms may vary, but if they are roughly in the middle of their Bibles, they should open to the Psalms.) Ask them to find the number of psalms in the book of Psalms. Invite them to read what is printed under the number of some of the psalms. Allow discussion.

3. Assign specific psalms to each student by having them select one of the slips of paper featuring a Psalm. Each slip of paper is a psalm that they must find, read, and write a word or two about the feeling of the psalm. Print the words *praise, anger, sadness, fear,* and *thanksgiving* on newsprint or the chalkboard. Afterward, ask students to share their psalm number and the word they chose to describe it. Ask for discoveries they made about the psalms.

4. Tell students that through the years one psalm has been the favorite of many people when they are in trouble or when they are sad. Read Psalm 23 together. Ask why they think that psalm would make people feel better.

5. *Closing:* Close with a prayer asking for God to listen to all of our feelings.

Parents' Question: What is your favorite psalm? Give each student a slip for parents to sign.

Psalm 1
Psalm 5
Psalm 13
Psalm 27
Psalm 33
Psalm 51
Psalm 111
Psalm 121
Psalm 138
Psalm 140
Psalm 150

LESSON 11

The wisdom of Solomon— Proverbs

Focus: The wisdom of Solomon—Proverbs

Scripture: Proverbs 1:1-8 and selected verses

Connections: Students will discuss what wisdom is, learn of King Solomon and his wisdom, and take selected Proverbs and turn them into learnings for their lives today.

Material Needed: Bibles, copies of "Proverbs: Words of Wisdom" (page 51), pencils, parent signature slips.

Activities:

1. *Opening:* **Ask students: If you could ask God for one thing, what would it be?** Allow each student to answer. Tell them there once was a king whose name was Solomon who asked God for one thing—that was wisdom. What is wisdom? ("good sense: judgment, a wise attitude or course of action"—*Merriam Webster Dictionary*). Collect parent signature slips.

2. King Solomon wrote many wise sayings to help his son learn. Ask students why they need to learn anything. Ask them how they learn (examples: reading, listening to parents, experiencing, studying, etc.). Record their answers on newsprint or chalkboard.

3. Divide students into groups of two or three depending on class size. Give each group a copy of "Proverbs: Words of Wisdom." Ask everyone to find Proverbs in their Bible. Assign the first four proverbs listed on the sheet to group 1, the second four to group 2, etc. Have each group look up their assigned proverbs and write what they think each proverb means. Tell students that these words of advice that King Solomon gave to his son are words that will help us today. Help them with words they may not understand. Allow about 15 minutes for this activity. (Note: Alter the number of proverbs according to the size of the class and the number of groups.)

4. Invite each group to share at least one of the proverbs in their own words with the whole group.

5. Closing: Pray for wisdom each day to help us to learn from parents, teachers, each other, and God.

Parents' Question: What is the best piece of advice you received to help you live a better life? Give each student a slip for parents to sign.

Proverbs

10:1	15:3	21:30
11:13	15:30	22:2
12:1	16:24	22:6
12:18	19:5	23:12
12:22	19:20	27:2
14:21	20:11	29:11
	21:3	29:17

LESSON 12
Review

Focus: Old Testament Review

Connections: Students will work in peer learning groups to review the information about the Old Testament.

Activities:

Note: This is a different kind of review. It is not a test like students have taken before. It is a peer learning experience in which students work together to enhance each other's learning. They will work in teams. Each team will have an opportunity to review each segment of the information on the Old Testament by going to a specific station and doing what they are told to do in the envelope provided. Ask students to open each envelope, read the instructions, and do what is required. When they have completed their task, they will raise their hands. You will check the accuracy of their task. If it is accurate, students will place all of the materials back into the envelope and move on to the next empty station. You will need one extra envelope than you have teams.

1. Divide your class into five teams of two to four students, depending on the size of the class. Copy and cut pages 54-58 and place each section in an envelope. Tell students that there are instructions of what to do and papers to work on in each envelope. Read the instructions carefully. The teacher(s) may need to explain each envelope before the

activity begins. Set the envelopes at different stations around the room. Send one team of students to each envelope, leaving one envelope free for any team that has nowhere to go next. Assure teams that everyone on each team will have an opportunity to complete a task.

2. Plan a celebration snack of animal crackers and juice. Invite students to find "two" of the animal crackers they will have to eat.

Materials Needed: A copy of "Old Testament Review" (pages 54-58), scissors, six (or more depending on the size of class) envelopes, snack. Copy and cut pages 54-58 and place each section in an envelope. Arrange the room in six or more stations.

Old Testament Review

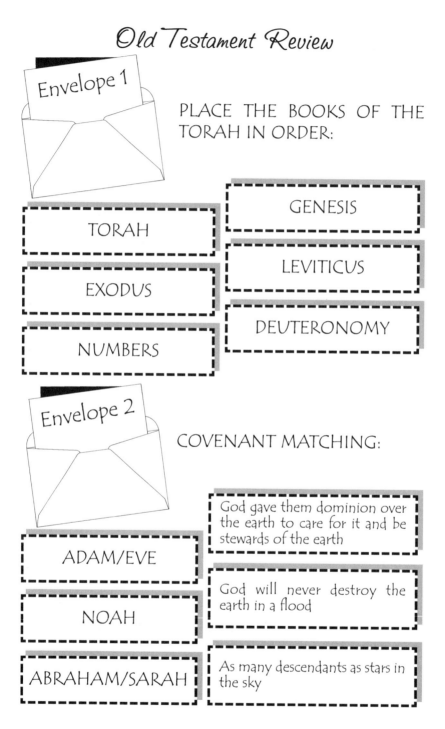

Envelope 1

PLACE THE BOOKS OF THE TORAH IN ORDER:

TORAH

EXODUS

NUMBERS

GENESIS

LEVITICUS

DEUTERONOMY

Envelope 2

COVENANT MATCHING:

ADAM/EVE

NOAH

ABRAHAM/SARAH

God gave them dominion over the earth to care for it and be stewards of the earth

God will never destroy the earth in a flood

As many descendants as stars in the sky

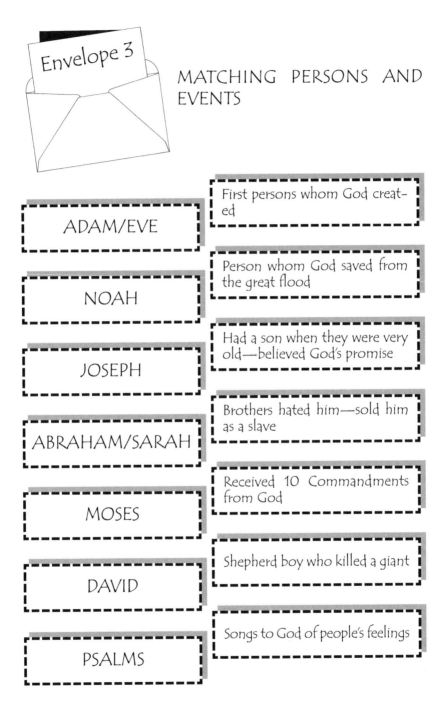

Envelope 3

MATCHING PERSONS AND EVENTS

ADAM/EVE	First persons whom God created
NOAH	Person whom God saved from the great flood
JOSEPH	Had a son when they were very old—believed God's promise
ABRAHAM/SARAH	Brothers hated him—sold him as a slave
MOSES	Received 10 Commandments from God
DAVID	Shepherd boy who killed a giant
PSALMS	Songs to God of people's feelings

Envelope 4

PLACE THE WORDS IN ORDER TO MAKE A SCRIPTURE VERSE — CHECK YOUR ANSWER BY READING JOHN 1

IN   THE   AND   WAS

WITH   AND   BEGINNING   WORD   THE

WAS   GOD.   WORD   THE   WORD

THE   GOD   WAS

Envelope 5

MATCH THE DAYS OF GOD'S CREATION WITH WHAT WAS CREATED

DAY 1	Day and Night
DAY 2	Sky
DAY 3	Earth/Seas/Plants
DAY 4	Sun/Moon/Stars
DAY 5	Birds/Fish
DAY 6	Animals and People
DAY 7	God Rested

Envelope 6

PLACE THE STATEMENTS
UNDER TRUE OR FALSE

TRUE	FALSE

THERE ARE 59 BOOKS IN THE BIBLE

THE BIBLE IS DIVIDED INTO TWO PARTS
OLD/NEW TESTAMENT

THE BIBLE BEGAN BY PEOPLE
WRITING STORIES AGAIN AND AGAIN

THE BIBLE IS THE STORY OF
GOD'S CONNECTION WITH HUMANS

THE BIBLE CONTAINS MANY DIFFERENT
KINDS OF BOOKS

THE BIBLE BEGAN BY TELLING STORIES
AGAIN AND AGAIN

THE BIBLE HAS 66 BOOKS

ABRAHAM AND SARAH
HAD MANY CHILDREN

DAVID WAS A SAILOR

DAVID PRACTICED USING HIS SLING
TO PROTECT HIS SHEEP

JOSEPH TOLD HIS BROTHERS
ABOUT HIS DREAMS

GOD TOLD NOAH THE WORLD WOULD BE
DESTROYED BY A FLOOD

GOD GAVE COMMANDMENTS TO OBEY
TO JOSEPH

ONE OF THE COMMANDMENTS IS TO
HONOR YOUR MOTHER AND FATHER

ONE OF THE COMMANDMENTS IS
TO LOVE GOD

THE PSALMS ARE SONGS TO GOD

GOD CREATED HUMANS IN GOD'S IMAGE

PART 3

The Christian/New Testament Teaches Us How to Live

LESSON 13

The Christian or New Testament

Focus: The Christian or New Testament

Scripture: Luke 1:1-4

Connections: Students are introduced to the Christian or New Testament.

Materials Needed: Bibles, newsprint/markers or chalkboard/chalk, a room or space large enough for students to run, parents signature slip.

Activities:

1. *Opening:* Ask: **What have you gotten recently that is new? Tell me how you feel when you get something new.** Invite discussion.

2. Look at the table of contents in your Bible. **Say: In this lesson we will begin to look at the Christian or New Testament today. Why do you think we needed a New Testament? What do you think are the differences between the Old/Hebrew and New/Christian Testaments?** Ask students to find the New Testament in the table of contents of their Bibles. Ask students to name the first four books of the New Testament. Repeat them together: Matthew, Mark, Luke, and John. Ask if anyone

knows what these books are called. **Say: They are known as the Gospels. "Gospel" means the teachings of Jesus or "the good news."** Ask why they think the gospel is good news.

3. Select one large uninterrupted wall in your room (or go into a hallway). Tell students that one corner edge (far left) of the room is when God created the world and the other corner edge (far right corner of the same wall) is today. Ask them to point to where, in this time span, they think Jesus lived on earth. Let all the students guess. Then show them that Jesus lived on earth about three inches from the end of the wall (far right) that is today. Everything else happened before that time.

4. Play "4 Square." Gather the students in the middle of a room where they can run. Tell them which corner is Matthew, which corner is Mark, which is Luke, and which is John. Select someone to be "It." That person must close his or her eyes while all the other students run to one of the four corners. After a count of 10, "It" calls out one of the names of the Gospels. All the students who are in that corner must sit down. The rest gather in the center of the room with a new person being "It." The game continues until all players are out. While students are seated, go over with them again the names of the four Gospels.

5. *Closing:* Close with a prayer thanking God for sending us Jesus to teach us.

Parents' Question: Can you name the first four books of the New Testament and what they are called? Give each student a slip for parents to sign.

LESSON 14
A child is born

Focus: A child is born

Scripture: Matthew 1:18-25; 2:1-12; Luke 2:1-20

Connections: Students will read the two accounts of the birth of Jesus and retell the story using props.

Materials Needed: Bibles, a copy of "The Birth of Jesus—Matthew and Luke" (page 65) for each student, pencils, paper, nativity set with only the pieces mentioned in Scripture (you will need one piece [example—Mary, Joseph, etc.] of the set for each child; for a large group, divide the students into teams with each team choosing a piece), a bag, parent signature slips.

Activities:
1. *Opening:* Ask students what they do in their family to remember Jesus' birth at Christmas. Allow ample time for each student to reply. Collect parent signature slips.

2. Ask students if they know the two stories of Jesus' birth. Explain that Matthew and Luke both tell of the birth of Jesus, but they tell the story in different ways. Ask students to find Matthew, the first book of the New Testament, and read Matthew 1:18-25 and 2:1-12. Invite

students to read the Scripture accounts. Make a list of the things mentioned in this story. Then ask them to locate Luke 2:1-20. Invite someone to read this account. Make a list of the things mentioned in this story. Ask students to comment on the similarities and differences in the stories. Give each student a copy of the diagram of "The Birth of Jesus." Have them record all the things that are in both stories in the center and all the things in Matthew's story on the side marked **Matthew**, and all the things in Luke's story on the side marked **Luke**. Allow time for students to write items.

3. Place the pieces from the nativity set into the bag. Have each child or group select a piece from the bag. Allow time for them to think about how to tell their part of the story. Ask them to line up in the order of the events that took place in the story. Make allowances for the time differences in Matthew and Luke. Ask the students which pieces are missing. Ask them why they are not included in this story. Help them to see that the Bible does not specifically mention many things that we take for granted (example—there is no mention of a donkey or camels or how many wise men there were).

4. *Closing:* End with a prayer for Jesus to be born in our hearts again and again.

Parents' Question: Can you tell the two stories of Jesus' birth? Give each student a slip for parents to sign.

The Birth of Jesus—Matthew and Luke

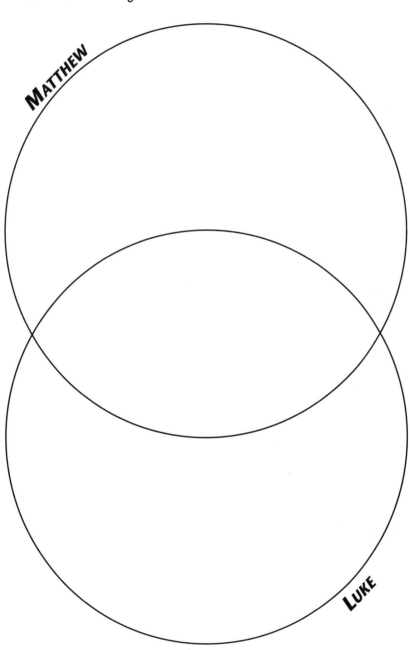

MATTHEW

LUKE

LESSON 15
The baptism of Jesus

Focus: The baptism of Jesus

Scripture: Matthew 3:13-17; Mark 1:9-11; Luke 3:21-22

Connections: Students will read the story of Jesus' baptism and connect it with either their own baptism or one they've witnessed.

Materials Needed: Bibles, newsprint/markers or chalk/chalkboard, map of the region of Judea, masking tape, shell (or bowl), water, parent signature slips.

Activities:

1. *Opening:* Ask students to tell you all the things they can do with water. Record answers on chalkboard or newsprint. Focus their attention on cleansing. Ask the children what "baptism" means. Encourage answers and make sure that everyone is aware that, for us, baptism means being cleansed and welcomed into the church. Collect parent signature slips.

2. Ask them if they were baptized and what their parents have told them about their baptism. Invite students to share their stories. If there are students who are not baptized, include them in the conversation by asking them what they remember about seeing a child being baptized.

3. Ask for volunteers to read the story of Jesus' baptism from Matthew's Gospel. Show students a map of Judea so they can see the River Jordan. Make it clear to the children that Jesus was an adult, probably about thirty years old. Explain that Jesus went into the water and was submerged. Help the children to understand that Jesus was baptized by John the Baptist (you may need to explain who John was). On newsprint or chalkboard create two columns headed SIMILAR and DIFFERENT. Ask how Jesus' baptism was similar to/different from their baptisms. List the responses in each column.

4. Show the children the water and the shell (or bowl). Explain that the shell is our symbol of baptism. As the children watch, pour a small amount of water into the shell. Invite the children to come to you and place their fingers into the water. Tell them to touch their hearts or their heads to symbolize how they would like to be clean and pure for God.

5. *Closing:* Close with a prayer thanking God for giving us baptism to wash ourselves clean for God.

Parents' Question: Do you know where Jesus was baptized, how old he was, and who baptized him? Give each student a slip for parents to sign.

LESSON 16
The temptations of Jesus

Focus: The temptations of Jesus

Scripture: Matthew 4:1-11; Mark 1:12-13; Luke 4:1-13

Connections: Students will learn about temptation, talk about a time they have been tempted, and read and discuss the three temptations of Jesus.

Materials Needed: Bibles, pencils, paper, S.T.O.P. sign language handout (page 70), parent signature slips.

Activities:

1. *Opening:* Ask students what "temptation" means. After you have a definition that everyone can understand, ask the students if they have ever been tempted. Ask what they did in that situation. Collect parent signature slips.

2. Invite a volunteer to read the first temptation from Matthew 4:1-4. Discuss what the Bible means by "Man cannot live by bread alone." **Say: What does it mean to live on the word of God? Wouldn't you get hungry?** Then have someone read Matthew 4:5-7. Discuss the scripture to help the students understand what it means to "not put the Lord your God to the test." Ask if they have ever *tested* God (example: God, I promise to come to

Sunday school every week if you help me pass my math test). Continue by inviting the reading of Matthew 4:8-11. Discuss the last temptation and what it means. Ask where the scripture says to "Worship the Lord your God and serve only him!" Ask who else they might worship (example—maybe they spend too much time on sports or video games, etc.; explain that this is not true worship, and then ask if it is what they love to do more than anything). Review the Ten Commandments. Ask which commandment Jesus was quoting in this passage.

3. Invite the students to tell the story of the temptations of Jesus in their own words. Invite them to draw a picture or write the temptations in their own words.

4. *Closing:* Close by teaching students the S.T.O.P. prayer to use when they are tempted to do something they are not sure is the right thing to do. Teach them sign language for S, T, O, P. Repeat the prayer while signing the letters.

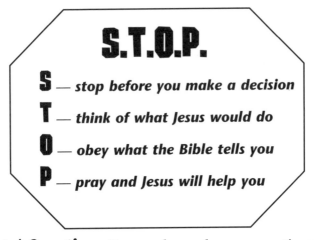

S.T.O.P.

S — *stop before you make a decision*

T — *think of what Jesus would do*

O — *obey what the Bible tells you*

P — *pray and Jesus will help you*

Parents' Question: Do you know how many times Jesus was tempted, by whom, and what the temptations were? Give each student a slip for parents to sign.

S.T.O.P.

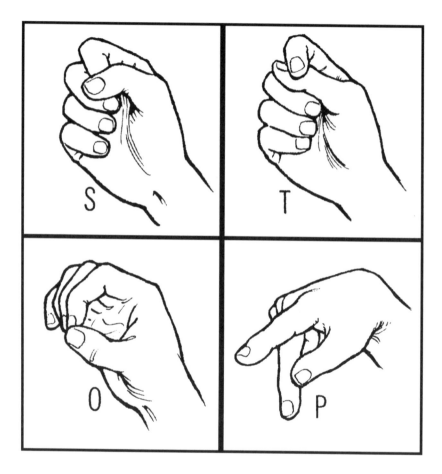

LESSON 17

Jesus calls his disciples and us

Focus: Jesus calls his disciples and us

Scripture: Matthew 4:18-22; Luke 5:2-11; John 1:35-42

Connections: Students will explore the meaning of the word *disciple,* name the first disciples Jesus called, experience the story through visual imagery, and play a game to enhance the learning of the names of the first disciples.

Materials Needed: Magnet(s), several metal objects, chalk/chalkboard or newsprint/markers, Bibles, paper, markers, masking tape, parent signature slips.

Activities:

1. *Opening:* Invite each student to use the magnet and see how it attracts metal objects. Write the word *charisma* on newsprint or chalkboard and discuss what it means. Tell the students that Jesus had charisma—like the magnet, he drew people to him. People chose to follow him and his teachings because there was a power that radiated from him that made them want to be with him. Collect parent signature slips.

2. Write the word *disciple* on newsprint or the chalkboard. Ask if students know the meaning of the word. Explain that *disciple* means "a person who follows a special

71

teacher." Ask if any of the students are disciples. Ask if they know the name of the special teacher the biblical disciples were following.

3. Ask if any students have been to a lake. Invite discussion of what lakes look and feel like. Ask students to listen while you read a story that took place near a lake. Read Matthew 4:18-22. Ask the students to listen to the story again, this time with their eyes closed. Ask them to picture the story as they hear it. Read the scripture again. Then ask, "What did you see as I read the story?" Invite responses from all students. Then ask, "What did you hear?" Again invite responses. Ask, "Why do you think these men left their fishing to follow Jesus?" Tell them that this was at the beginning of Jesus' ministry. He was not yet well known. Remind the students of the magnet.

4. Play "4 Corners." Write the names Peter, Andrew, James, and John on pieces of paper. Tape one name to each of the four corners of the room. Invite someone to stand in the center of the room. That person closes his or her eyes and counts slowly to ten. The other students go to one of the corners of the room. The person in the center, with eyes still closed, calls out one of the four disciples' names. All the students in that corner must sit down. The game continues until one person is left standing. That person moves to the center and the game begins again. If no one is left standing, select a new person to stand in the center of the room.

5. *Closing:* Pray that we may be willing followers of Jesus and his teachings.

Parents' Question: What do *disciple* and *charisma* mean? Can you name the first four disciples of Jesus? Give each student a slip for parents to sign.

LESSON 18

Prayer and the Lord's Prayer

Focus: Prayer and the Lord's Prayer

Scripture: Matthew 5:6-14; Luke 11:2-4

Connections: Students will discuss the many aspects of prayer (ACTS) and retell the Lord's Prayer in their own words.

Materials Needed: Bibles, the Lord's Prayer written on sheet of newsprint (leave space between each line to record students' words), marker, paper, pen, parent signature slips.

Activities:
1. *Opening:* Ask students if they pray, when they pray, where they pray, and how they pray. Ask them to say the Lord's Prayer. Collect parent signature slips.

2. Talk about the different kinds of prayer:
   - *Adoration* (praising/honoring God)
   - *Confession* (telling God we are sorry for the wrong things we've done)
   - *Thanksgiving* (thanking God)
   - *Supplication* (praying for others)

   Discuss opportunities for each of the different kinds of prayer. Practice each kind of prayer—praising God,

73

thanking God, praying for others out loud, and confessing things we've done silently.

<u>***or***</u>

Teach children the "Hand Prayer." Hold your left hand up with thumb pointing to yourself and spread your fingers. Together say,

Thumb (points to yourself)—Pray for yourself, that you might be kind and considerate of others.

Pointer finger—(points to others—sometimes in love, sometimes in anger)—Pray for others around you.

Tall finger—(symbolizes people who are bigger than you)—Pray for teachers, leaders of your church and school, leaders of our country.

Ring finger—(symbolizes a direct link to your heart)—Pray for those you love.

Pinky finger—(reminds us of those who are small or in need)—Pray for those who have less than you.

3. Invite the children to turn to Matthew 6:5 and read aloud the scripture. Ask how it is like the prayer we pray in church. Are there differences?

4. Invite the children to explain in their own words what each line of the Lord's Prayer means. Record their version of the Lord's Prayer and type it for each of them for the next class.

5. *Closing:* Say the Lord's Prayer together.

Parents' Question: What do the words of the Lord's Prayer mean to you? Give each student a slip for parents to sign.

LESSON 19

Jesus performs a miracle and teaches us to share

Focus: Jesus performs a miracle and teaches us to share

Scripture: John 6:1-14; Matthew 14:13-21; Mark 6:30-40; Luke 9:10-17

Connections: Students will experience sharing, read the story of the miracle of feeding the five thousand, and make coupons that tell about their own sharing.

Materials Needed: One apple, a knife, napkins, a map of biblical times, *New Adventure Bible,* one sharing coupon per student (page 77), parent signature slips.

Activities:

1. *Opening:* Show the students the apple and talk about being hungry. Ask if anyone would mind if you ate the apple right now. As children react, ask, "How can I share? There's only one apple." Invite ideas on how to share the apple. Cut the apple and give each student a piece. Talk about how they felt about your not sharing. Collect parent signature slips.

2. Invite students to read the story of feeding the five thousand from John's Gospel. Ask when they have been part of a large crowd of people. Read the story again, stopping

appropriately. Ask the students to become the boy in the story. Then ask:

- How do you think Jesus fed so many people with just your lunch?
- What made you come to be a part of the five thousand people who were listening to Jesus?
- What made you want to share your food with Jesus' friends?
- How does it feel when you share something of yours?

3. Have children turn to the map in the back of the *New Adventure Bible* that shows "Jesus' Ministry." Help children to locate where the feeding took place. Show them the Sea of Galilee.

4. Distribute Sharing Coupons. Instruct children to fill in one coupon each time they share something this week, and tell them that we will discuss their sharing in the next meeting.

5. *Closing:* Close with prayer thanking God for Jesus' miracles and for teaching us to share.

Parents' Question: Tell me a time when you shared something. What happened because of it? Give each student a slip for parents to sign.

Sharing Coupon

I shared _____

with _____

on _____

I felt _____.

Name _____

Sharing Coupon

I shared _____

with _____

on _____

I felt _____.

Name _____

LESSON 20
Jesus heals

Focus: Jesus heals

Scripture: Mark 2:1-12; Matthew 9:1-8; Luke 5:27-32

Connections: Students will learn about Jesus' healing powers through having heard and retold the story of the healing of the paralytic.

Materials Needed: Bibles, picture of a home in biblical times showing a thatched roof, copies of "The Healing of the Paralytic" (page 80), parent signature slips.

Activities:

1. *Opening:* Ask: **When have you helped a friend? When have you been helped by a friend?** Invite discussion and ask what it felt like to help or be helped. Collect parent signature slips.

2. Read the story of the healing of the paralytic in the three Gospels. Compare the stories. Ask why they think the same story is told three times. Ask how they think it was possible for Jesus to heal someone.

3. Look at the picture of a home in biblical times. Tell students how it was possible to lower a man through the roof.

4. Distribute copies of "The Healing of the Paralytic." Let them color the picture and write the story in their own words at the bottom of the page.

5. *Closing:* Close with a prayer about helping and healing.

Parents' Question: Why was a man lowered through a roof so Jesus could heal him? Give each student a slip for parents to sign.

LESSON 21

God celebrates
when the lost is found

Focus: God celebrates when the lost is found

Scripture: Luke 15:1-7; Matthew 18:12-14

Connections: Students will encounter having lost something and the joy of finding it, and they will relate that joy to God's joy when a sinner repents.

Materials Needed: Bibles, keys, coin, broom, a snack for each student, parent signature slips.

Activities:

1. *Opening:* As students enter, tell them you have lost your keys and ask them to help you find them. (Hide the keys well enough to make it possible, but not too easy, to find them.) When the keys have been found, tell the students how relieved you are and offer them a snack to celebrate. As you are munching, ask if they have ever lost anything and how they felt when it was found. Collect parent signature slips.

2. Tell them that in the next three lessons we will be learning about something called "parables." Explain that a parable is a short story with one message and is usually told in word pictures to make it easy to understand. Tell

them that Jesus did much of his teaching in parables because they taught a lesson using things that people were familiar with, like sheep, seeds, travelers, and coins. Explain that many of the people could not read or write and these stories helped them to understand Jesus' message. **Say: The first parable is about sheep. Find Luke 15 in your Bible.** Invite someone to read Luke 15:1-2. Ask, "Why do you think the Pharisees and scribes were upset that Jesus was eating with sinners? Who is a sinner today?" Then read Luke 15:4-7.

3. **Say: Listen to the parable again and see if you can discover what Jesus was saying about sinners.** Invite discussion. Ask someone to read Luke 15:8-10. Invite students to act out the parable of the lost coin. (If several respond and you have time, let them act it out more than once.) Ask, "What is the message about sinners in the story of the lost coin? Why do you think Jesus told two parables about the same thing?"

4. So far Jesus has talked about sheep and coins. Ask, "How do you think God feels about people who sin? Let's find out what Jesus said in the third parable about being lost." Invite someone to read Luke 15:11-31. Ask students who represented God in the story. Ask, "How did the father react when his son, who was a lost sinner, came home? How do you think God feels when we say we are sorry for the things we have done wrong?"

5. *Closing:* Close with a prayer about being sorry for the things we have done wrong and helping God to celebrate when we are forgiven.

Parents' Question: What is a parable? Why did Jesus use parables to teach? Give each student a slip for parents to sign.

LESSON 22

Who is my neighbor?

Focus: Who is my neighbor?

Scripture: Luke 10:25-37

Connections: Students will create a modern-day parable of the good Samaritan.

Materials Needed: Bibles, map (or maps in students' Bibles), a copy of the story grid on page 85 and "Modern-Day Good Samaritan" on page 86 for each group of two students, pencils, chalk/chalkboard or newsprint/markers, parent signature slips.

Activities:

1. *Opening:* Ask students to tell you the names of their best friends. **Say: If your best friend was in trouble, how would you help?** Allow time for discussion. Then ask, "Is there someone you don't like very well?" Allow for discussion. Then ask, "If the person you don't like was in trouble, what would you do?" Allow time for discussion. Then say, "Jesus tells us the answer to this question in the parable of the good Samaritan." Collect parent signature slips.

2. Introduce the characters by writing them on a chart—the traveler (making a long journey between two cities by walking some rough roads), the robbers (who knew this

was a busy highway for business travelers and found a place to hide until the attack), the priest (a holy man who would be unclean if he touched a dead or dying man), a Levite (an assistant to the priests in the Temple, who would also be unclean if he touched someone dead or dying), a Samaritan (Samaria was an area not far from Jerusalem, and the people from Samaria and the Jewish people from Jerusalem did not like each other; they were enemies). Ask if there are questions and repeat the character descriptions if necessary.

3. Invite students to find Luke 10:25-37. Ask someone to read the parable of the good Samaritan out loud while the rest of the class follows along in their Bibles.

4. Invite students to work in pairs. Give each pair of students a copy of the story grid, and ask them to circle one person from each column to create their own parable of the good Samaritan using the "Modern-Day Good Samaritan." Allow students about six or seven minutes to create their stories. Invite volunteers to share their story time with the class. Allow enough time for every pair of students that chooses to share their parable.

5. *Closing:* Lead a prayer asking God to help us be good neighbors, even to those that we don't like very much.

Parents' Question: Who did Jesus say is our neighbor? Give each student a slip for parents to sign.

84

To create a modern-day telling of the story of the good Samaritan, please select and circle one item from each of the lists in the story grid. When you have finished this task, write your choices from each column in the blank lines on page 86.

STORY GRID

TRAVELER	TO/FROM	1ST PERSON	2ND PERSON	3RD PERSON	ACTION
rock star	Buffalo/ Rochester	principal	tv cameraman	garbage collector	took to hotel
single mother	Dallas/ Houston	musician	business person	cab driver	took to hospital
teacher	Hollywood/ Los Angeles	undertaker	minister	plumber	took home
nurse	Memphis/ Nashville	lawyer	runaway kid	street gang member	took to clinic
police officer	Atlanta/ Montgomery	doctor	movie star	teen playing hockey	took to police station

Modern-Day Good Samaritan

A _____ (Traveler) was traveling

to_____ (To)

from _____ (From)

when _____ (Traveler)

was attacked by robbers. They beat _____

_____(Traveler) up and left the person

by the roadside. A _____(1st Person)

passed by and kept on going. Then a _____

_____(2nd Person) arrived and did not stop

but moved on quickly. Finally a _____

(3rd Person) came by, stopped, helped _____

_____(Traveler) into his car and

_____ (Action).

Who was the neighbor?

LESSON 23

The parable of the sower

Focus: The parable of the sower

Scripture: Mark 4:1-9, 13-20 (Matthew 13:1-9; Luke 8:1-4)

Connections: Students will read the parable of the sower, discuss their understanding of the parable, make a shoebox story, and plant seeds to grow and transplant outside.

Materials Needed: Bibles, a shoebox for each child, enough soil/stones/weeds for each box, cups, soil for planting, seeds for planting, water, table covering, parent signature slips.

Activities:

1. *Opening:* Ask students if they have ever planted seeds. Ask what it takes to make seeds grow (sun, soil, water, etc.). Collect parent signature slips.

2. Invite students to read the parable in Mark's Gospel (4:1-9). Discuss what they think the parable means. Then have them read Mark 4:13-20 to see if they were right in their understanding.

3. Give each student a shoebox, soil, seeds, weeds, and stones for creating a diorama (i.e., a three-dimensional scene inside the box). Lay the box inside the box top so the top projects out like a porch. Place soil along the bottom of the box. Arrange stones on the left side, weeds in

the center, and several seeds on the right side. Place the remainder of the seeds on the stones and weeds. Use large seeds (like sunflowers) so they can be seen. Invite the children to retell the story as they create their scene.

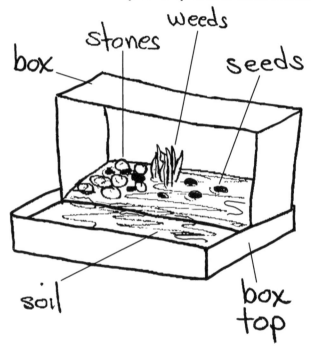

4. Give each child a cup with soil and a seed. Help them to plant the seed, water it, and place it in a sunny spot in the room. **Say: We'll check the seeds each week, and when it gets warm enough and the plants are big enough, we can plant them outside.**

5. *Closing:* Close with a prayer about God planting seeds in our hearts of wanting to know Jesus and his teachings.

Parents' Question: Do you know the parable of the sower and what it means? Give each student a slip for parents to sign.

LESSON 24

Palm Sunday—
the triumphant entry
into Jerusalem

Focus: Palm Sunday—the triumphant entry into Jerusalem

Scripture: Luke 19:28-40 (Matthew 21:1-11; Mark 11:1-11; John 12:12-19)

Connections: Students will read and experience the story of Palm Sunday in a variety of ways.

Materials Needed: Bibles, copies of "Jesus' Entry into Jerusalem" (page 91), palm fronds, a fist-sized stone for each student, markers, parent signature slips.

Activities:

1. *Opening:* **Say: How many of you have been to a parade? What was it like?** Invite discussion. Collect parent signature slips.

2. **Say: We're going to read about an event like a parade that Jesus took part in.** Find Luke 19. Now find verse 28. Give each student a copy of "Jesus' Entry into Jerusalem" to look at and color. Read the story (verses 28-40) and discuss any words or phrases that are unfamiliar.

3. Distribute palm fronds for the students to see and touch. Ask why they think people waved palms fronds. (Palm

trees are prevalent in Israel, and waving palm fronds was a sign of reverence.) Invite students to roleplay Jesus' entry into Jerusalem. Have different people play the crowd, the disciples, and Jesus.

4. Give each student a fist-sized stone and markers. Invite students to decorate their stones with a face, being as creative as they can in expressions, facial features, and hair. Explain Jesus' comment to the Pharisees in Luke 19:40. Nothing can stop God's Word. Remind the students to write their names on the bottom of the stones. Line the stones up on the altar or along the main aisle of the sanctuary.

5. *Closing:* Close with prayer about spreading Jesus' word.

Parents' Question: What does it mean for the stones to cry out? Give each student a slip for parents to sign.

Jesus' Entry into Jerusalem

LESSON 25
Holy Thursday

Focus: Holy Thursday

Scripture: Luke 22:1-65 (Matthew 26; Mark 14)

Connections: Students will hear and retell in words and pictures the story of the events of Holy Thursday.

Materials Needed: Bibles, newsprint/markers or chalk-board/chalk, paper, parent signature slips.

Activities:

1. *Opening:* Invite students to talk about a special meal in their homes when family and friends came together (examples—Thanksgiving, Christmas, birthdays, etc.). Ask why this time is special. Why is it important to share a meal with special friends and family? Collect parent signature slips.

2. Tell the story of Holy Thursday from a combination of the Gospel accounts. Be sure to include:

   • the gathering in the upper room
   • the Passover meal
   • Jesus prediction of Peter's denial
   • Jesus praying at Gethsemane

- Judas' betrayal of Jesus
- Jesus' arrest
- Jesus before the high priests
- Peter's denial

Tell the story in your own words. Periodically stop during your storytelling and ask how they think Jesus felt and how the different characters felt. Allow for questions and clarification.

3. Distribute paper and markers to each student. Ask the students to repeat the story to you. Write the most important parts on the chalkboard or newsprint. Divide the story according to how many students you have and invite each of them to draw his or her part of the story and place it in sequence. You might want to have your students tell the story using the pictures they have created as part of the worship service for Holy Thursday.

4. *Closing:* Close with prayer to remember Jesus each time we receive Holy Communion.

Parents' Question: What happened the night before Jesus died? Give each student a slip for parents to sign.

LESSON 26
Good Friday

Focus: Good Friday

Scripture: Matthew 27:1-61; Mark 15:1-47; Luke 23:1-56; John 18:19-40; 19:1-42

Connections: Students will read the story of the trial, persecution, crucifixion, and burial of Jesus. They will retell the story by finding the answers to specific questions and comparing the story in all four Gospels.

Materials Needed: Bibles, pencils, a copy of "Scriptural Accounts of Jesus' Death" (page 96) for each group of four students, parent signature slips.

Activities:
1. *Opening:* Ask students if they know what happened on Good Friday. Ask them why they think it is called Good Friday when that is the day that Jesus died. Provide several "right answers." Collect parent signature slips.

   - It was originally called God's Friday, and the name changed over the years.
   - Even though Jesus died, it was good for us because he died for our salvation.

2. Divide the students into four groups. Distribute copies of "Scriptural Accounts of Jesus' Death" to each group. Invite each group to select one passage and read the scripture together. Then ask each group to answer the questions about the scriptures. Allow approximately fifteen minutes for reading and researching. (Note: The amount of time needed will vary depending on the age and reading abilities of the students.) Gather the whole group together and read the answers to the questions.

3. *Closing:* Close with prayer about Jesus' suffering and dying for us.

Parents' Question: Why do you think Good Friday is called Good Friday? Give each student a slip for parents to sign.

Scriptural Accounts of Jesus' Death

Matthew 27:1-66
Luke 23:1-56   **Mark 15:1-47**
John 18:19-40; 19:1-42

Read one of the above Scripture passages and find the answers to these questions:

Jesus was taken to be tried before _____, the Roman governor.

The prisoner whom Pilate set free instead of Jesus was named _____.

The soldiers made fun of Jesus and gave him a _____ and a _____.

_____ was the Cyrene man who helped Jesus carry the cross.

They crucified Jesus in a place called _____.

Soldiers threw _____ to see who would win Jesus' robe.

_____ men were crucified along with Jesus.

Jesus died at _____ o'clock.

A man named _____ buried Jesus in a tomb he had made for himself.

LESSON 27
The Easter story

Focus: The Easter story

Scripture: Matthew 28:1-10; Mark 16:1-10; Luke 24:1-12; John 20:1-10

Connections: Students will hear and participate in a litany telling the Easter story.

Materials Needed: Bibles, copies of "Litany: The Story of Easter Morning" (page 99) for each student, paper, Folded Cross (page 100), and scissors for each student, parent signature slips.

Activities:
1. *Opening:* Say: **What is the most amazing story you have ever heard? Did you believe it when you first heard it? How did you react?** Collect parent signature slips.

2. Distribute copies of "Litany: The Story of Easter Morning." Invite one of the students to read the litany aloud. The rest of the class will participate with the litany response (in caps).

3. Invite the students to tell the story in their own words.

4. Help students to create a Folded Cross. Work together. Do each step slowly. Provide help as needed.

5. *Closing:* Close with a prayer about being an Easter People who believe that because Jesus died for us and was not in the tomb, that we have hope.

LITANY: The Story of Easter Morning

After the sabbath, at dawn on the first day of the week, Mary Magdalene and the other Mary went to look at the tomb.

HE IS NOT HERE—HE HAS RISEN.

There was a violent earthquake, for an angel of the Lord came down from heaven and, going to the tomb, rolled back the stone and sat on it. His appearance was like lightning, and his clothes were white as snow.

HE IS NOT HERE—HE HAS RISEN.

The guards were so afraid of him that they shook and became like dead men.

HE IS NOT HERE—HE HAS RISEN.

The angel said to the women, "Do not be afraid, for I know that you are looking for Jesus, who was crucified. He is not here; he has risen, just as he said."

HE IS NOT HERE—HE HAS RISEN.

Come here and see the place where he lay.

HE IS NOT HERE—HE HAS RISEN.

Then go quickly and tell his disciples: "He has risen from the dead and is going ahead of you into Galilee. There you will see him." Now I have told you.

HE IS NOT HERE—HE HAS RISEN.

So the women hurried away from the tomb, afraid yet filled with joy, and ran to tell his disciples.

HE IS NOT HERE—HE HAS RISEN.

Suddenly Jesus met them. "Greetings," he said. They came to him, clasped his feet, and worshiped him.

HE IS NOT HERE—HE HAS RISEN.

Then Jesus said to them, "Do not be afraid. Go and tell my brothers to go to Galilee; there they will see me."

HE IS NOT HERE—HE HAS RISEN. CHRIST THE LORD IS RISEN TODAY. AMEN!

Folded Cross

Directions:

Take an 8 1/2" x 11" piece of white (typing) paper and lay it on the table surface lengthwise (11" up and down 8 1/2" across).

Take the upper right corner and fold it to meet the left edge (it will form a triangle with extra space on the bottom).

Take the upper left corner point and fold it across to the right edge (looks like a house with a pointed roof).

Fold the page in half with the folded edges inside.

Fold the edges to meet in the middle.

Cut in half from bottom to top lengthwise.

Open the larger (inside) piece to form a cross. Say: Ta Da!

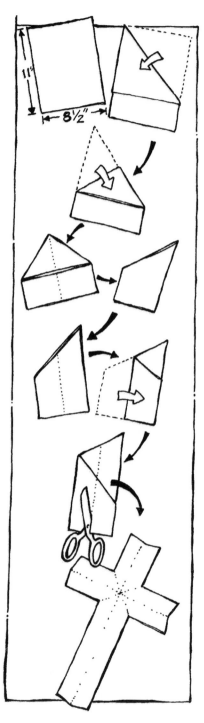

LESSON 28
The conversion of Saul

Focus: The conversion of Saul

Scripture: Acts 22:3-21

Connections: Students will become aware of who Saul/Paul was and how believing in Jesus can bring about change in a person.

Materials Needed: Bibles, paper plates and markers for each student, pre-recorded tape of Acts 22:3-21, tape player, posterboard, markers, parent signature slips.

Activities:
1. *Opening:* Ask students to find a partner and face that person. Have them look at each other for a full minute and take note of details. Afterward ask them to turn their backs to each other for another minute. During this minute have them change three things about their appearance (example—girls might reposition a barrette or rearrange their hair, turn up a collar, take off a bracelet, take off a sock, etc.; boys might take off a belt, unbutton a top shirt button, take off a watch, etc.). After a minute, have the partners face each other again and take turns to see if they can notice the changes that were made. (If the students like this, ask them to repeat the activity—chang-

ing three other things about their appearance). Ask what they noticed about changed appearances. Was it easy to see the changes made? Was it difficult? Why? Ask how we can tell when a person changes. Collect parent signature slips.

2. Give each student a paper plate and markers. Invite them to draw a happy face on one side of the plate and a sad face on the other side. When they have completed their drawings, explain that we are going to learn about an important man who changed his life and his name. He was a person who persecuted (explain the word) Christians and then became their greatest teacher and supporter. Play a tape of a reading of Acts 22:3-21. Ask students to show you the side of the face on the plate, happy or sad, that describes the way they feel as they listen to the story. Ask how they think someone could change so much. How can Jesus change our lives?

3. Ask the students to create a poster with words and pictures of things that can change in their lives when they listen to Jesus. Hang the poster in a hallway or on a bulletin board to share with your church.

4. *Closing:* End with a prayer about changing our lives because we follow Jesus.

Parents' Question: What has changed in your life because you follow Jesus? Give each student a slip for parents to sign.

LESSON 29

Paul was a missionary

Focus: Paul was a missionary and took several journeys to spread the word of Jesus

Scripture: Acts 14:21-23*

Connections: Students will discover what a missionary was during Jesus' lifetime and what a missionary is now. They will trace Paul's journeys and make discoveries about his travels and teachings.

Materials Needed: Bibles, map of your town or state, map of Paul's journeys (appears in the back of the *New Adventure Bible*, or if you are using a Bible without a map, locate a map of Paul's journeys from old curriculum or your church school files), newsprint/markers or chalkboard/chalk, parent signature slips.

Activities:
1. *Opening:* Open your map and ask students to find your town (or your street). Ask them how maps are helpful. Collect parent signature slips.

*The stories of Paul's missionary journeys occur in Acts 14–21. Leaders may want to familiarize themselves with the three journeys to help guide students through this lesson. The key point is that Paul traveled extensively, spreading the word of Jesus.

2. Look at the map of Paul's journeys. Ask students to make observations about what the map tells about Paul's journeys. **Say: How much information can you find?** (Example—three separate trips, one trip to Rome, traveled over water, visited lots of countries, went to some places two or three times.) Record their discoveries. Ask why they think he traveled so much. What was he doing?

3. Define *missionary*—one who is sent to do religious or charitable work in a territory or foreign country (*American Heritage Dictionary*). Tell the students that Paul was a missionary. He traveled all over the world that was known to them at the time, telling people about Jesus and his teaching. Ask if there are missionaries today. If your church or community sponsors missionaries, tell the students about them. Ask why they think missionaries might still be important.

4. Ask students how they can become missionaries.

5. *Closing:* Conclude with a prayer about spreading God's Word.

Parents' Question: What do you know about missionaries? Give each student a slip for parents to sign.

LESSON 30

Paul in prison

Focus: Paul in prison

Scripture: Acts 16:20-34

Connections: Students will again discover that God can take something bad and turn it into something good through faith.

Materials Needed: Bibles, paper, pencils, building blocks (borrowed from the nursery) or paper hung to look like a prison cell, parent signature slips. Pre-arrange a portion of your room (or another room) to look like a prison cell and plan to hold a portion of the lesson in this area. Also, pre-arrange for someone to break down the wall at a given signal when the earthquake is mentioned in Scripture.

Activities:

1. *Opening:* **Say: What's the worst thing that has happened to you?** Invite discussion. Tell them that Paul and his friend Silas were beaten and thrown into prison because they were teaching about Jesus. Ask students why they think Paul and Silas were put into prison for teaching about Jesus. Collect parent signature slips.

2. Ask students to bring their Bibles and lead them into the

prison cell. Sit on the floor and ask students to find Acts 16:20. Invite students to read of Paul's encounter in jail in Acts 16:20-24. Ask what they think it was like to be beaten and have their feet locked up. Ask what they would do if it happened to them. **Then say: Paul and Silas behaved very differently. Listen carefully to hear what they did.** Ask someone to read Acts 16:25. Ask, "If you were in prison and had been beaten, do you think you would sing?" Invite discussion. Invite another student to continue reading. As they begin to read Acts 16:26 have someone knock the building blocks down. Wait until the students regain their composure and read verse 28. Ask what they think will happen next. Invite another student to read through verse 34.

3. Ask what they think of this story. Have them return to their seats and write a brief account of what happened to Paul and Silas to share with their family.

4. *Closing:* Close with a prayer about praising God in the worst circumstances.

Parents' Question: What was the amazing thing that happened when Paul and Silas were in prison? Give each student a slip for parents to sign.

LESSON 31

The body of Christ

Focus: The body of Christ

Scripture: 1 Corinthians 12:12-27

Connections: Students will discover the importance of all the parts of the congregation—the body of Christ.

Materials Needed: Bibles, a copy of the "Gingerbread Body" (page 109) for each student, newsprint/marker or chalkboard/chalk, paper, and markers or pencils for notes or pictures, parent signature slips.

Activities:

1. *Opening:* Give each student a copy of the "Gingerbread Body." Ask them to write or share their favorite "head" activity, "hand" activity, "heart" activity, "foot" activity. Invite discussion on the different answers. Collect parent signature slips.

2. Invite volunteers to read 1 Corinthians 12:12-27. Assign *body parts* to students. One can be the hand, another the eye, the ear, the foot, the head, etc. If your class is large, extend the number of parts to left hand, nose, etc. Each student should have a part of the body. Ask them to imagine what it would be like if the whole person were just

their part. Could a hand eat? Where would the hand put the food? Invite them to see how silly this image is.

3. Tell them that the church is like that. Ask them what your church would be like if there was only singing or only the custodian or only the teachers. Explain that God and the church need each of us and our different gifts in order for the *body* to work well. Ask students to list all the important things that God needs us to do in the church. Record the list. Tell the students that Paul wrote this letter to the people so they would understand that all of them were important to the church and that no one was more important than anyone else.

4. Invite the students to write a note or draw a picture for someone in the church to say "Thank You" for his or her gifts that make the church work well.

5. **Closing:** Close with a prayer, thanking God for our differences.

Parents' Question: Why does God need people with different gifts in the church? Give each student a slip for parents to sign.

Gingerbread Body

LESSON 32
The greatest of these is love

Focus: The greatest of these is love

Scripture: 1 Corinthians 13

Connections: Students will explore the many sides of love.

Materials Needed: Bibles, newsprint/markers or chalkboard/chalk, a copy of the "Mind Map" on page 112 for each student, pencils, parent signature slips.

Activities:

1. *Opening:* Say: **Who loves you?** Record answers on newsprint or chalkboard. Then ask, "Who do you love?" Place checkmarks next to the answers that have already been recorded. Collect parent signature slips.

2. Read 1 Corinthians 13 by inviting students to take turns reading two or three verses. Provide explanations for unfamiliar words and phrases. Ask students to retell this passage in their own words. Record their version of 1 Corinthians 13 on newsprint.

3. Provide each student with a "Mind Map." Invite them to look at the map and find love at the center and how Paul defines love in the other circles. On each of the connect-

ing lines, ask them to write a word that will help them to know how they can live out that part of love at home, school, and church. When students have completed their Mind Maps, invite them to share. Acknowledge the many ways we can live love.

4. *Closing:* Conclude with a prayer, asking God to help us love those around us.

Parents' Question: Who loves you? Who do you love? Give each student a slip for parents to sign.

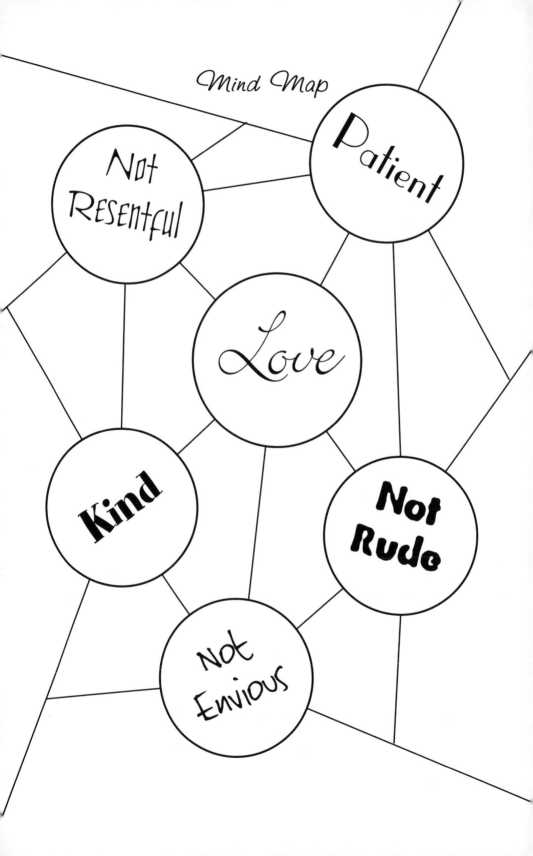

LESSON 33

Pentecost—
the birth of the church

Focus: Pentecost—the birth of the church

Scripture: Acts 2:1-12

Connections: Students will experience different languages and extend the message of Jesus beyond themselves.

Materials Needed: Bibles, "Jesus Loves You" slips (page 115), cupcakes (at least two per student—one to eat and one to give away), frosting, knives for spreading frosting. Cut a slit in each cupcake to make inserting the slips easier, parent signature slips.

Activities:
1. *Opening:* Invite students to say their names out loud, all together at the count of three. Next invite them to say their birthday, month and date (April 29) out loud, all at the same time at the count of three. Then ask them to say their teacher's name out loud, all at the same time at the count of three. Invite responses. Tell them this is what it must have sounded like on the day of Pentecost. Now ask them to say "Jesus" out loud at the same time at the count of three. **Say: This is what God wants from all those who believe in God and God's son, Jesus. God wants us to be together in praising and worshiping through Jesus.** Collect parent signature slips.

2. Ask students to find Acts 2. Tell them that the book of Acts was written by Luke. It is a story of what happened to the disciples after Jesus rose from the dead and went to be with God in heaven. Invite various students to read aloud Acts 2:1-12. Ask for their thoughts on how it must have felt to be a part of that group that day. Explain that hearing the message in different languages was a miracle. Tell them that in Acts 2:14-43 Peter gave a speech telling all the people about Jesus and his teaching. About three thousand people were baptized after that experience, and we consider the experience of Pentecost to be the birth of the church. From then on hundreds of people began living by and spreading Jesus' word.

3. Invite students to place a "Jesus Loves You" strip into their cupcakes. Have the students frost one cupcake for themselves and the other for someone in the church to spread the good news about Jesus. As they are frosting their cupcakes, ask who they will give the second one to and why they chose that person. Enjoy eating one cupcake as a celebration.

4. *Closing:* Close with a prayer about spreading the word of Jesus to everyone.

Parents' Question: Do you know what happened at Pentecost? Give each student a slip for parents to sign.

Jesus loves YoU	Jesus loves YoU
Jesus loves YoU	Jesus loves YoU
Jesus loves YoU	Jesus loves YoU
Jesus loves YoU	Jesus loves YoU
Jesus loves YoU	Jesus loves YoU
Jesus loves YoU	Jesus loves YoU
Jesus loves YoU	Jesus loves YoU
Jesus loves YoU	Jesus loves YoU
Jesus loves YoU	Jesus loves YoU
Jesus loves YoU	Jesus loves YoU
Jesus loves YoU	Jesus loves YoU
Jesus loves YoU	Jesus loves YoU
Jesus loves YoU	Jesus loves YoU
Jesus loves YoU	Jesus loves YoU
Jesus loves YoU	Jesus loves YoU

LESSON 34

Discovering what we have learned

Focus: Discovering what we have learned

Scripture: Deuteronomy 6:4-7

Connections: Students will have a chance to review, in fun and exciting ways, information they have learned in this class.

Materials Needed: Bibles, award certificate (page 119), pencils, newsprint/markers or chalkboard/chalk, "Smarties" candy for each student.

Activities:

Invite students to participate in as many of the activities as there is time for. Each activity will reinforce what students have learned in a fun and exciting way. Make this a time of celebration of what students have learned.

Invite them to share:

- Their favorite Bible story
- The most interesting thing they have learned
- A way that they act differently now because of learning about Jesus' teaching

_or_

Form them into two teams. Have them add the total number of brothers or sisters that they have. The team with the highest number of siblings goes first. Let them play a *Pictionary*-like game with their favorite Bible stories. Someone from the first team draws a picture depicting their favorite Bible story. The second team makes guesses based on the picture. If the second team gets the correct story, they then draw the next picture. Allow this to go on for about ten minutes.

<u>***or***</u>

Form them into two different teams. Invite each team to make up five questions from the Bible stories they've learned. Allow time to write questions. Have them count the number of people on their team who are wearing sneakers. The team with the most number of people wearing sneakers goes first. Each team gets to ask questions until someone from the opposing team doesn't know the answer or all five questions are answered.

<u>***or***</u>

Form them into two different teams. Have them count the number of people on their team wearing red. The team with the most red goes first. Invite them to play charades with Bible stories. The first team comes up with a Bible story and tries to communicate the story by having the other team guess based on silent clues. (Example: holding up one finger to show first word and then performing a task like searching around and sweeping to tell the events of the story.)

<u>*or*</u>

Have them write a letter to a friend telling them about Jesus and his teaching.

<u>*or*</u>

Provide each student with paper and markers. Ask them each to draw a picture of an event in the Bible. When they are finished, line the pictures in the order they happened and have students tell the story in each picture.

Award certificates of accomplishment to all students who participated in this class (in worship?) and invite the congregation to tell the students how proud they are of them.

Provide a snack of "Smarties" candy to celebrate!

Closing: Close with prayer for continued use of the Bible as a very special book to help you for the rest of your life.

- You might want to invite parents to this session to help celebrate.

Certificate

of

Accomplishment

This is to certify that

_____

has completed a course in

Bible Basics

1 *Parents' Question:* How many books are in the Bible?

Parents' Signature:_____

2 *Parents' Question:* Do you know what the Torah is? What are the names of the first five books of the Bible?

Parents' Signature:_____

3 *Parents' Question:* What did God create on each day?

Parents' Signature:_____

4 *Parents' Question:* What did Eve and Adam do to disobey God? What happened because they disobeyed?

Parents' Signature:_____

5 *Parents' Question:* What do you know about the story of Noah and the great flood?

Parents' Signature:_____

6 *Parents' Question:* What was special about the baby named Isaac who was born to Abraham and Sarah? What does "Isaac" mean?

Parents' Signature:_____

7 *Parents' Question:* Do you know the special gift that Joseph's father gave him?

Parents' Signature:_____

8 *Parents' Question:* Can you name the Ten Commandments?

Parents' Signature:_____

9 *Parents' Question:* How big is a cubit? Do you think David was brave or dumb to fight Goliath?

Parents' Signature:_____

10 *Parents' Question:* What is your favorite psalm?

Parents' Signature:_____

11 *Parents' Question:* What is the best piece of advice you received to help you lead a better life?

Parents' Signature:_____

13 *Parents' Question:* Can you name the first four books of the New Testament and what they are called?

Parents' Signature:_____

14 *Parents' Question:* Can you tell the two stories of Jesus' birth?

Parents' Signature:_____

15 *Parents' Question:* Do you know where Jesus was baptized, how old he was, and who baptized him?

Parents' Signature:_____

16 *Parents' Question:* Do you know how many times Jesus was tempted, by whom, and what the temptations were?

Parents' Signature:_____

17 *Parents' Question:* What do *disciple* and *charisma* mean? Can you name the four disciples of Jesus?

Parents' Signature:_____

18 *Parents' Question:* What do the words of the Lord's Prayer mean to you?

*Parents' Signature:*_____

19 *Parents' Question:* Tell me a time when you shared something. What happened because of it?

*Parents' Signature:*_____

20 *Parents' Question:* Why was a man lowered through a roof so Jesus could heal him?

*Parents' Signature:*_____

21 *Parents' Question:* What is a parable? Why did Jesus use parables to teach?

*Parents' Signature:*_____

22 *Parents' Question:* Who did Jesus say is our neighbor?

*Parents' Signature:*_____

23 *Parents' Question:* Do you know the parable of the sower and what it means?

*Parents' Signature:*_____

24 *Parents' Question:* What does it mean for the stones to cry out?

*Parents' Signature:*_____

25 *Parents' Question:* What happened the night before Jesus died?

*Parents' Signature:*_____

26 *Parents' Question:* Why do you think Good Friday is called Good Friday?

*Parents' Signature:*_____

27 *Parents' Question:* Why is it important to our faith that Jesus rose from the dead?

*Parents' Signature:*_____

28 *Parents' Question:* What has changed in your life because you follow Jesus?

*Parents' Signature:*_____

29 *Parents' Question:* What do you know about missionaries?

*Parents' Signature:*_____

30 *Parents' Question:* What was the amazing thing that happened when Paul and Silas were in prison?

*Parents' Signature:*_____

31 *Parents' Question:* Why does God need people with different gifts in the church?

*Parents' Signature:*_____

32 *Parents' Question:* Who loves you? Who do you love?

*Parents' Signature:*_____

33 *Parents' Question:* Do you know what happened at Pentecost?

*Parents' Signature:*_____

Scripture Index

OLD TESTAMENT

NEW TESTAMENT